THE POSITIVE PSYCHOLOGY FOR DAILY JOY

MASTER GRATITUDE AND MINDFULNESS, BREAK FREE FROM NEGATIVITY, REWIRE YOUR MIND FOR SUCCESS, AND TRANSFORM EVERY DAY INTO PURE JOY

PREM SAGAR SUNCHU

YOUR FREE GIFT !!

As a token of my thanks for taking out time to read my book, I would like to offer you a **Free-Gift**:

Click the Below Link and Download your **Free eBook PDF**.

"Bridges to Happiness: Stories and Wisdom from Around the World"

ABOUT THE AUTHOR

Prem Sagar Sunchu, the Accomplished Author of "The Positive Psychology for Daily Joy"

Meet **Mr. Prem Sagar**, an ordinary soul born in the vibrant city of Secunderabad, India, where the tapestry of life weaves stories of resilience and dreams. His journey is a testament to the power of perpetual learning, where every encounter is a lesson, and every moment holds the potential for growth.

A man of many dimensions, Mr. Sagar embodies the qualities of a perpetual student, a dedicated listener, and a dreamer who gazes at the stars but keeps his feet firmly grounded. His aspirations soar high, and his relentless pursuit of them is fueled by a genuine desire to make a positive impact on those around him.

Having served as a Chief Manager in the prestigious State Bank of India, Mr. Sagar brings a wealth of experience from the world of banking. However, for him, retirement isn't a conclusion but a commencement—a reminder that life's true journey begins when one can reflect on the wisdom gained from the first innings.

In Mr. Sagar's view, retirement is not a retreat but a stepping stone to a realm of infinite possibilities. It's an opportunity to surpass the ordinary, where the canvas of life awaits new brushstrokes of creativity and purpose. For him, the "be good and do good policy" isn't just a mantra; it's a guiding principle that shapes his approach to life.

As he embraces the second innings, Mr. Sagar encourages others to view retirement not as a winding down but as a springboard to new endeavors. It's a time when accumulated wisdom meets fresh energy, and the monotony of routine gives way to the vibrancy of creativity. His belief is clear: retirement is not just a number; it's a chapter where the richness of experience meets the possibilities in abundance.

In the world of Mr. Prem Sagar, retirement is not a period of rest but a canvas waiting to be painted with the colors of newfound wisdom, creativity, and a different outlook on life.

Prem Sagar Sunchu
M.Com, LLM, Certified Independent Director (IICA)
GOI,
Author, Sole Arbitrator and Legal Consultant, Freelancer

ACKNOWLEDGEMENTS

In profound gratitude, I extend heartfelt appreciation to my amazing parents. To my caring and resilient mother, **Smt. S.L. Lakshmi**, who gracefully navigated the challenges of my father's service transfers, made countless sacrifices to bind our family together. My father, **Shri S.R. Lakshman Rao**, stands as my enduring role model—his post-retirement vibrancy, marked by a dedicated hobby of reading and writing, serves as the very foundation that propels me into the realm of authorship. A debt of gratitude is owed to my beautiful wife, **Smt. S.P. Padma Sree** is a constant source of inspiration, unwavering strength, and invaluable guidance. Balancing family responsibilities and the intricate path of an author, her presence has been the foundation of my journey.

To my handsome sons, **S.P. Gautam Sagar**, **S.P. Prayag Sagar**, and **S.P. Akshaj Sagar**, whose unwavering support and responsibility bear testament to the great strength they provide. Their motivation fuels my endeavors across all the diverse traits I undertake.

I owe thanks to **Mr. Som Bathla**, an **Amazon #1 Best-selling** author, for his mentorship, motivation, and guidance in the realms of **Writing, Self-Publishing, and Launching Books**. His support has been instrumental in initiating my journey as an Authorpreneur.

My Sincere thanks to **Mr. Sooraj Achar**, who is also an Amazon Bestselling Author, for his **Professional Editing,** Formatting, and Publishing support.

In acknowledging these pillars of support, I am reminded that the tapestry of my life and authorial pursuit is woven with threads of love, sacrifice, and inspiration. With profound thanks to my family, who stand as my bedrock of strength and motivation.

DEDICATION

To the guiding stars of my universe—my Parents, Grandparents, Parents-in-law, Brothers, Sisters, the cherished members of our extended Family and Friends. Their unwavering support and boundless encouragement have been the driving force behind my Author Journey.

In the tapestry of my life, each of them has woven threads of inspiration and resilience, transforming mere words into stories and dreams into realities. Their confidence in me has been a constant source of strength, propelling me forward through the path of this journey.

With heartfelt gratitude, I dedicate the pages of my work to the pillars of love and encouragement that they are, recognizing that every word I pen is a tribute to the collective spirit of our family. May this dedication reflect the depth of my appreciation for the profound impact they have had on my creative journey.

"The Positive Psychology of Daily Joy" is my second book in the series of five books- **"The Happiness Mastery."**

CONTENTS

INTRODUCTION: THE POWER OF POSITIVE PSYCHOLOGY IN EVERYDAY LIFE

"Happiness is not something ready-made. It comes from your own actions." — Dalai Lama

Introduction: The Joyful Revolution

In a world dominated by endless to-do lists, societal pressures, and the relentless pursuit of success, happiness often seems elusive. Yet, groundbreaking advancements in the field of positive psychology have revealed that joy is not a fleeting emotion reserved for special occasions. Instead, it is a learnable skill and a daily practice. Positive psychology, the scientific study of human flourishing, empowers individuals to shift their focus from life's obstacles to its possibilities.

Consider the story of Rachel, a single mother juggling a demanding job and raising two kids. Overwhelmed and burnt out, Rachel decided to try a 30-day gratitude challenge after reading about its psychological benefits. By consciously noting three things she was grateful for each day, Rachel experienced a profound shift in her mindset. She found herself smiling more, connecting better with her children, and handling stress with newfound resilience. Rachel's transformation exemplifies how small, intentional actions rooted in positive psychology can spark a joyful revolution.

This chapter delves into how positive psychology can enhance daily life, why practices like gratitude and mindfulness are vital, and how breaking free from negativity can set the stage for sustained happiness. Along the way, you'll discover actionable insights, backed by science and relatable real-life examples, to inspire your journey toward lasting joy.

Understanding Daily Joy: Why Gratitude, Mindfulness, and Positivity Matter

1. The Science Behind Gratitude

Research consistently shows that gratitude is a cornerstone of emotional well-being. A 2003 study by Emmons and McCullough revealed that participants who kept gratitude journals experienced higher levels of optimism and physical health compared to those who focused on daily hassles. Gratitude not only uplifts our spirits but also rewires the brain. Neuroscientists have found that expressing gratitude activates the brain's reward system, increasing the production of dopamine and serotonin, the chemicals responsible for happiness.

Take the example of Jake, a software engineer struggling with workplace dissatisfaction. After introducing a daily gratitude practice, Jake started appreciating small wins—like his team's camaraderie or completing a challenging task. This mental shift not only improved Jake's mood but also enhanced his productivity and relationships with colleagues.

Actionable Step: Begin a gratitude journal. Each night, write down three things that went well during the day and reflect on why they mattered. Over time, this practice can reframe your perspective and cultivate a more positive outlook.

2. The Role of Mindfulness in Daily Joy Mindfulness, the art of being fully present in the moment, is another transformative tool. A 2011 study published in *The Journal of Positive Psychology* highlighted that people who practice mindfulness report higher levels of life satisfaction and emotional stability. Mindfulness mitigates the stress caused by overthinking and anchors us in the present, where joy resides.

Take Priya's story, for instance. A busy marketing executive, Priya often found herself distracted during family dinners, scrolling through work emails. After attending a mindfulness workshop, she committed to unplugging during meals and practicing deep breathing exercises. This simple shift enriched her family connections and helped her savor moments she previously overlooked.

Actionable Step: Incorporate a mindfulness minute into your routine. Pause once a day to take five deep breaths, noticing the sensations in your body and the environment around you. This simple practice can ground you in the present and increase your capacity for joy.

3. The Positivity Bias: Rewiring the Brain Our brains are hardwired for negativity, a survival mechanism from our evolutionary past. However, cultivating positivity is entirely possible. Studies by Barbara Fredrickson, a leading positive psychology researcher, show that positive emotions broaden our thought-action repertoires, encouraging creativity, resilience, and stronger social bonds.

Fredrickson's "Broaden-and-Build" theory explains how positive emotions like joy, love, and contentment expand our mental and physical resources, enabling us to build enduring skills and relationships. For example, a simple act of kindness—like offering a genuine compliment—can create a ripple effect of positivity in your life and others'.

Actionable Step: Practice "Three Good Things" daily. Before bed, recall three positive experiences from your day and reflect on what made them special. This practice can rewire your brain to focus on the good, fostering long-term positivity.

Breaking the Negativity Cycle: A Roadmap for Lasting Happiness

Breaking free from negativity requires intentional effort and a commitment to change. Consider this metaphor: negativity is like a heavy backpack filled with stones. Each negative thought or habit adds another stone, weighing you down. Positive psychology offers tools to lighten the load.

1. Identifying and Reframing Negative Thoughts

A 2010 study published in *Cognitive Therapy and Research* found that cognitive reframing—challenging negative thoughts and replacing them with constructive alternatives—can significantly reduce anxiety and depression. For example, instead of thinking, "I always fail," reframe it as, "I've faced challenges before and learned from them."

Actionable Step: Keep a "Thought Journal." When a negative thought arises, write it down, identify its trigger, and brainstorm a more positive reframe. Over time, this practice can weaken negativity's grip.

2. The Power of Community

Surrounding yourself with positive, supportive individuals is crucial. A Harvard study spanning over 80 years found that the quality of relationships is the single most significant predictor of happiness. By fostering connections with people who uplift and inspire you, you create a buffer against negativity.

Actionable Step: Dedicate time each week to nurturing meaningful relationships. Whether it's a coffee date with a friend or a heartfelt phone call, these moments build your joy reserves.

3. Digital Minimalism for Mental Clarity Emerging trends like digital minimalism emphasize reducing screen time to enhance mental well-being. Excessive social media use is linked to increased anxiety and comparison. By setting boundaries, you reclaim time and energy for more fulfilling activities.

Actionable Step: Implement a "Tech-Free Hour" daily. Use this time to engage in offline hobbies, connect with loved ones, or simply enjoy solitude. This practice fosters clarity and reduces stress.

What Awaits You in This Book: A Sneak Peek into the Journey

This book equips you with the tools to harness the power of positive psychology and transform your daily life. From cultivating gratitude and practicing mindfulness to breaking free from negativity, each chapter offers actionable strategies, relatable stories, and research-backed insights. Here's what you can look forward to:

1. **Practical Tools:** Learn simple, effective habits to boost your joy.

2. **Inspiring Stories:** Discover how real people have overcome challenges and found happiness.

3. **Interactive Elements:** Engage with habit trackers, journaling prompts, and reflection exercises.

4. **Emerging Trends:** Explore fresh perspectives, like digital minimalism and habits for remote workers.

Conclusion: Tying It All Together

Positive psychology is more than a field of study; it's a way of life. By integrating gratitude, mindfulness, and positivity into your daily routine, you can unlock a wellspring of joy that transcends life's challenges. Rachel's and Jake's stories show that happiness isn't about perfection but progress. With the actionable steps outlined in this chapter, you're equipped to start your own joyful revolution today.

Remember, the journey to lasting happiness begins with a single step—whether it's writing in a gratitude journal, practicing a mindfulness minute, or reframing a negative thought. Take that step now, and watch as the ripple effects of positivity transform your life and the lives of those around you.

Resources for Further Reading

1. Emmons, R. A., & McCullough, M. E. (2003). "Counting Blessings Versus Burdens: An Experimental Investigation of Gratitude and Subjective Well-Being." *Journal of Personality and Social Psychology.*

2. Fredrickson, B. L. (2001). "The Role of Posi-

tive Emotions in Positive Psychology: The Broaden-and-Build Theory." *American Psychologist.*

3. Kabat-Zinn, J. (1994). *Wherever You Go, There You Are: Mindfulness Meditation in Everyday Life.*

4. Newport, C. (2019). *Digital Minimalism: Choosing a Focused Life in a Noisy World.*

5. Lyubomirsky, S. (2007). *The How of Happiness: A New Approach to Getting the Life You Want.*

6. Seligman, M. E. P. (2011). *Flourish: A Visionary New Understanding

CHAPTER 1

CULTIVATING GRATITUDE—THE FOUNDATION OF JOY

"Acknowledging the good that you already have in your life is the foundation for all abundance." — *Eckhart Tolle*

Introduction: Gratitude—A Simple Shift, A Profound Transformation

Life often feels like an endless treadmill—we hustle for promotions, juggle personal obligations, and scroll through curated social media feeds, all while searching for a deeper sense of fulfillment. Amid this chaos, gratitude offers a transformative practice—a chance to pause, reflect, and appreciate the richness of our lives. Research and countless real-life examples reveal that gratitude is more than a feel-good sentiment; it is a scientifically validated method to boost mental well-being, resilience, and overall happiness.

Consider the story of Elena, a high-achieving entrepreneur whose life looked enviable from the outside. Despite her success, she struggled with anxiety and dissatisfaction. On the advice of a friend, she started a gratitude journal, listing three positive moments from her day each night. Within weeks, her perspective began to shift. She noticed more joy in small, everyday moments, from a stranger's smile to her morning coffee. Elena's story is not unique. Gratitude has the power to transform lives by fostering a mindset focused on abundance rather than lack.

In this chapter, we explore the profound science behind gratitude, practical steps to incorporate it into your daily life, and how this simple habit can serve as the foundation for sustained joy. Let's dive deeper into the world of gratitude and uncover its life-altering potential.

The Science of Gratitude: How It Rewires Your Brain

Gratitude is not just a warm, fuzzy feeling; it's a neurological powerhouse. Studies in neuroscience reveal that practicing gratitude stimulates the brain's reward centers, particularly the medial prefrontal cortex. This rewiring enhances our capacity for happiness and emotional resilience.

Research Spotlight

In a groundbreaking study by Emmons and McCullough (2003), participants who kept weekly gratitude journals reported higher levels of optimism, physical health, and life satisfaction. Neuroscientists further explain that expressing gratitude increases dopamine and serotonin levels—neurotransmitters responsible for feelings of happiness.

Another study by Fox et al. (2015) used fMRI scans to observe brain activity in participants who engaged in gratitude exercises. The findings revealed enhanced neural sensitivity in the anterior cingulate cortex and medial prefrontal cortex, areas associated with decision-making and emotional regulation.

Real-Life Impact

Consider Sam, a recent college graduate navigating the stress of job rejections. Feeling stuck, he joined a gratitude workshop where he practiced reflecting on three things he appreciated daily. Over time, Sam noticed a shift—he became more optimistic and resilient, focusing on his strengths rather than his setbacks. Gratitude not only improved his mental outlook but also motivated him to keep pursuing his goals.

Actionable Takeaway

Start with a simple gratitude habit: each night, jot down three things you're grateful for. Focus on specific moments, like a supportive conversation or a delicious meal, and reflect on why they mattered.

Gratitude in Action: Transforming Challenges into Opportunities

Life's challenges often obscure the good in our lives, but gratitude offers a lens to reframe adversity. This mindset doesn't deny hardship but instead highlights opportunities for growth and connection hidden within difficulties.

Story: Turning Loss into Strength

A powerful example is the story of Maya, who faced the devastating loss of her partner. Struggling to find meaning, she began a daily gratitude practice, starting with small things like a sunny day or the kindness of friends. Over time, this habit helped Maya reframe her grief. Instead of dwelling solely on her loss, she began cherishing the love and memories she shared with her partner. Gratitude didn't erase her pain but provided a pathway to healing and resilience.

Scientific Perspective

Gratitude's role in resilience is backed by research. A study published in Behavior Research and Therapy (2010) found that individuals practicing gratitude were better equipped to manage stress and recover from trauma. This emotional strength stems from gratitude's ability to foster optimism and strengthen social bonds.

Actionable Takeaway

Use gratitude as a reframing tool during challenges. When faced with adversity, ask yourself: What lesson can I learn from this? Who supported me during this time? Write down these reflections to reinforce your sense of gratitude.

Daily Practices: Simple Gratitude Rituals for a Happier You

Incorporating gratitude into your routine doesn't require significant time or effort. Simple, consistent practices can yield profound results.

Rituals to Begin Today

1. Morning Gratitude Affirmations: Start your day by stating three things you're grateful for. This sets a positive tone for the day ahead.

2. Gratitude Jar: Keep a jar where you write down one positive moment each day. Review these notes at the end of the month to reflect on your blessings.

3. Gratitude Walks: Combine mindfulness and gratitude by taking a walk and focusing on the beauty around you—the sound of birds, the warmth of the sun, or the kindness of a passerby.

Emerging Trends

- Digital Gratitude Apps: Apps like Gratitude and Presently offer guided prompts and reminders, making it easier to build a daily habit.

- Gratitude for Remote Workers: In virtual settings, gratitude can strengthen team bonds. For instance, dedicating a few minutes during meetings for team members to share what they appreciate fosters connection and positivity.

Actionable Takeaway

Choose one gratitude ritual and practice it for 30 days. Consistency is key to embedding gratitude into your daily life.

Gratitude Journaling: A 5-Minute Habit That Yields Lifetime Benefits

Journaling is one of the most effective tools for cultivating gratitude. By reflecting on specific moments of gratitude, you're training your brain to notice and savor positive experiences.

How to Get Started

- Keep It Simple: Dedicate a notebook solely for gratitude journaling.

- Be Specific: Instead of writing, "I'm grateful for my family," try, "I'm grateful for my sister's support during my presentation today."

- Reflect on the Why: Explore why each item on your list is meaningful to deepen the emotional impact.

Real-Life Story

Jason, a middle school teacher, struggled with burnout. He started a gratitude journal, noting three moments of joy from his day, such as a student's enthusiasm or a kind note from a colleague. This 5-minute habit transformed Jason's outlook, helping him reconnect with his passion for teaching and approach challenges with a renewed perspective.

Scientific Insight

Lyubomirsky (2007) notes in The How of Happiness that journaling boosts positive emotions and reduces depressive symptoms. The act of writing helps solidify positive experiences in our memory, making them more impactful.

Actionable Takeaway

Set aside five minutes each evening to write in your gratitude journal. Focus on three specific experiences from your day, reflecting on their significance and emotional impact.

Conclusion: Gratitude—Your Gateway to Joy

Gratitude is not a fleeting act but a powerful habit that rewires your brain, reframes challenges, and enriches your daily life. Whether you're starting with a gratitude journal, affirmations, or mindful walks, the key is consistency. The stories of Elena, Sam, Maya, and Jason illustrate how gratitude can transform perspectives and strengthen resilience, even in adversity.

By weaving gratitude into your life, you're laying the foundation for sustained joy. Start small, stay committed, and watch as gratitude unlocks a world of abundance and happiness.

Resources for Further Reading

1. Emmons, R. A., & McCullough, M. E. (2003). "Counting Blessings Versus Burdens: An Experimental Investigation of Gratitude and Subjective Well-Being." Journal of Personality and Social Psychology.

2. Fox, G. R., Kaplan, J., Damasio, H., & Damasio, A. (2015). "Neural Correlates of Gratitude." Frontiers in Psychology.

3. Lyubomirsky, S. (2007). The How of Happiness: A New Approach to Getting the Life You Want.

4. Kabat-Zinn, J. (1994). Wherever You Go, There You Are: Mindfulness Meditation in Everyday Life.

5. Newport, C. (2019). Digital Minimalism: Choosing a Focused Life in a Noisy World.

6. Fredrickson, B. L. (2001). "The Role of Positive Emotions in Positive Psychology: The Broaden-and-Build Theory."

CHAPTER 2

MINDFULNESS FOR A CALM AND PRESENT MIND

"Feelings come and go like clouds in a windy sky. Conscious breathing is my anchor." —
Thich Nhat Hanh

Introduction: Finding Calm Amid Chaos

In today's fast-paced, distraction-driven world, our minds are often preoccupied with what lies ahead or what has already passed. This constant mental chatter not only robs us of peace but also diminishes our ability to experience life fully. Mindfulness, the practice of living in the present moment with awareness and without judgment, offers a transformative antidote. It's a powerful tool to calm the chaos and connect deeply with ourselves and others.

Consider the story of Mia, a young professional navigating the relentless pressures of her corporate job. Mia found herself perpetually anxious, unable to switch off her racing thoughts even at night. A chance encounter with a mindfulness coach led her to begin practicing simple breathing exercises. Within weeks, Mia noticed a profound change. She could handle stress more gracefully, enjoy moments of peace, and strengthen her relationships by being truly present. Her story exemplifies the profound impact mindfulness can have on transforming daily life.

This chapter delves into the essence of mindfulness, actionable practices for cultivating it, and strategies for overcoming the common pitfalls of overthinking and disconnection.

What Is Mindfulness?: The Art of Living in the Now

Mindfulness is the practice of bringing one's attention to the present moment with curiosity and acceptance. It's not about stopping thoughts but observing them without becoming entangled. Jon Kabat-Zinn, the pioneer of modern mindfulness, defines it as "paying attention in a particular way: on purpose, in the present moment, and nonjudgmentally."

Scientific studies validate the profound benefits of mindfulness. A 2011 study published in *Psychiatry Research: Neuroimaging* found that participants who engaged in an eight-week mindfulness-based stress reduction (MBSR) program showed increased gray matter density in areas of the brain associated with learning, memory, and emotional regulation.

Mindfulness doesn't require hours of meditation or retreating from daily responsibilities. It's a skill that can be woven into everyday activities like eating, walking, or even washing dishes. The key lies in intentionality and presence.

Mindful Practices for Daily Joy: Breathing, Observation, and Awareness

1. Conscious Breathing: The Anchor of Presence

Breathing is a natural and accessible tool for cultivating mindfulness. When stress or overwhelm arises, focusing on the rhythm of your breath can ground you in the moment.

- **Practice:** The 4-7-8 Technique

    a. Inhale deeply through your nose for a count of 4.

    b. Hold your breath for a count of 7.

    c. Exhale slowly through your mouth for a count of 8. Repeat this cycle three times to calm the nervous system and regain focus.

2. Observing the World with Fresh Eyes

Mindfulness encourages us to experience our surroundings with a beginner's mind—noticing details often overlooked in the rush of life.

- **Practice:** Nature Observation Spend five minutes outdoors focusing on a single element—a flower, a tree, or the sky. Pay attention to its colors, shapes, and textures. This practice fosters a sense of wonder and connection to the present.

3. Cultivating Awareness in Everyday Tasks

Simple daily activities offer opportunities for mindfulness. For example, when eating, notice the texture, taste, and aroma of each bite. When walking, focus on the sensation of your feet touching the ground.

Overcoming the Overthinking Trap: Techniques for Mental Clarity

Overthinking is a pervasive issue that clouds judgment and exacerbates anxiety. Mindfulness equips us with tools to break free from this mental loop.

1. Labeling Thoughts

Instead of resisting intrusive thoughts, acknowledge them with labels such as "worrying," "planning," or "remembering." This practice creates distance between you and your thoughts, reducing their power.

- **Practice:** Thought Journal At the end of the day, jot down recurring thoughts or worries. Reflect on their triggers and whether they're rooted in reality or assumptions. This process fosters awareness and helps reframe unproductive patterns.

2. Grounding Exercises

Grounding involves redirecting attention to physical sensations to anchor yourself in the present.

- **Practice:** The 5-4-3-2-1 Technique

- Identify 5 things you can see.

- Name 4 things you can touch.

- Listen for 3 sounds.

- Notice 2 smells.

- Focus on 1 taste. This exercise interrupts over-thinking and reconnects you with the now.

3. Letting Go Through Meditation

Meditation teaches acceptance of thoughts without clinging or aversion. Over time, it strengthens mental clarity and resilience.

- **Practice:** Body Scan Meditation Spend 10 minutes scanning your body from head to toe, noticing areas of tension or relaxation. This practice cultivates awareness and deepens the mind-body connection.

Mindful Relationships: Building Deeper Connections Through Presence

Relationships thrive on presence. Mindfulness enhances our ability to listen, empathize, and respond authentically, fostering deeper bonds.

1. Active Listening

Mindful listening involves giving full attention to the speaker without planning your response or interrupting. It's about hearing not just words but emotions and intentions.

- **Practice:** The Pause and Reflect Technique When someone speaks, pause for a moment before responding. This creates space to absorb their message fully and reply thoughtfully.

2. Practicing Empathy

Mindfulness strengthens empathy by encouraging us to see situations from another's perspective.

- **Practice:** Loving-Kindness Meditation

  ○ Close your eyes and take a few deep breaths.

  ○ Visualize someone you care about and silently repeat, "May you be happy. May you be healthy. May you be at peace." Extend these wishes to yourself, acquaintances, and eventually, all beings.

3. Creating Tech-Free Zones

Distractions from devices often hinder meaningful interactions. Establishing boundaries for screen use can enhance the quality of relationships.

- **Practice:** Device-Free Dinners Commit to sharing meals without phones or other screens. Use this time to engage in genuine conversations and connect deeply with loved ones.

Real-Life Story: The Transformation of Alex

Alex, a graphic designer, struggled with overthinking and disconnection from his family. His evenings were spent either ruminating about work or scrolling through social media. After attending a mindfulness workshop, Alex began practicing conscious breathing and setting aside a tech-free hour each evening. Within weeks, he noticed a dramatic improvement in his mood and relationships. He became more present with his kids, engaging in activities that brought them closer. Mindfulness not only reduced Alex's stress but also enriched his family life.

Conclusion: Living with Awareness

Mindfulness is a gateway to a calmer, more fulfilling life. By practicing presence, we can navigate challenges with grace, deepen our relationships, and savor life's ordinary moments. Whether through conscious breathing, grounding exercises, or active listening, mindfulness offers practical tools to transform the way we experience the world.

As you embark on your mindfulness journey, remember that it's not about achieving perfection but cultivating awareness one moment at a time. Commit to small, consistent practices, and watch as they ripple through every aspect of your life, bringing clarity, connection, and calm.

Resources for Further Reading

1. Kabat-Zinn, J. (1994). *Wherever You Go, There You Are: Mindfulness Meditation in Everyday Life.*

2. Hanson, R., & Mendius, R. (2009). *Buddha's Brain:*

The Practical Neuroscience of Happiness, Love, and Wisdom.

3. Harris, D. (2014). *10% Happier: How I Tamed the Voice in My Head.*

4. Siegel, D. J. (2010). *The Mindful Brain: Reflection and Attunement in the Cultivation of Well-Being.*

5. Nhat Hanh, T. (1975). *The Miracle of Mindfulness: An Introduction to the Practice of Meditation.*

6. Williams, M., & Penman, D. (2011). *Mindfulness: An Eight-Week Plan for Finding Peace in a Frantic World.*

7. Fredrickson, B. L. (2009). *Positivity: Top-Notch Research Reveals the Upward Spiral That Will Change Your Life.*

8. Newport, C. (2019). *Digital Minimalism: Choosing a Focused Life in a Noisy World.*

CHAPTER 3

BREAKING FREE FROM NEGATIVITY

"You cannot have a positive life with a negative mind." —Joyce Meyer

Introduction: The Heavy Backpack of Negativity

Negativity can feel like an invisible weight that we carry through life, affecting our decisions, relationships, and mental health. It often manifests as self-doubt, unproductive habits, or toxic thought cycles that cloud our ability to experience joy. While some negativity serves as a survival mechanism, over time, it can become a habitual mindset that limits personal growth.

Consider the story of Anna, a high-achieving lawyer who constantly battled self-critical thoughts. Despite her professional success, Anna struggled to find satisfaction, often replaying past mistakes and fearing future failures. It wasn't until she identified her negative patterns and implemented actionable strategies that Anna began to experience freedom from her mental burdens. Her transformation illustrates that breaking free from negativity isn't just possible—it's life-changing.

This chapter explores how to recognize and dismantle negative thought patterns, reframe perspectives, detox the mind, and create environments that nurture positivity. By adopting these practices, you can free yourself from negativity and unlock a path to sustained happiness.

Identifying Negative Patterns: Awareness Is the First Step

The first step to overcoming negativity is recognizing its presence. Negative thought patterns often operate beneath the surface, shaping our emotions and behaviors in subtle but profound ways.

Common Negative Patterns

1. Catastrophizing: Expecting the worst-case scenario in every situation.

2. Overgeneralization: Drawing sweeping conclusions based on isolated incidents.

3. Mental Filtering: Focusing exclusively on the negative aspects of an experience.

The Science of Awareness

Research published in Behavior Research and Therapy (2006) shows that becoming aware of thought patterns is crucial for disrupting their influence. Awareness creates a psychological distance that allows individuals to challenge and replace negative thoughts.

Actionable Step: Start a "Thought Diary." Spend five minutes daily jotting down recurring negative thoughts, their triggers, and your emotional response. Over time, you'll uncover patterns that need addressing.

Reframing Your Perspective: Turning Obstacles into Opportunities

Reframing involves consciously shifting how we interpret challenges. Instead of seeing obstacles as barriers, reframing teaches us to view them as opportunities for growth.

The Power of Reframing

A study by Dr. Martin Seligman, a pioneer in positive psychology, demonstrates how optimistic reframing can lead to improved resilience and overall well-being. When individuals reframe setbacks as temporary and solvable, they're better equipped to bounce back.

Real-Life Example

Mark, a small business owner, faced a major setback when his startup failed. Instead of dwelling on the failure, Mark reframed it as a learning experience. He analyzed what went wrong, sought mentorship, and launched a second business that thrived. Mark's success underscores the power of perspective.

Actionable Step: Practice "Cognitive Reappraisal." When faced with a challenge, ask yourself: "What can I learn from this?" and "How can I grow because of this experience?"

Detox Your Mind: Practical Steps to Let Go of Toxic Thoughts

Letting go of toxic thoughts is akin to decluttering your mind. Just as a clean environment promotes clarity, a clear mind fosters joy.

Techniques for Mental Detox

1. Meditation: A study in JAMA Internal Medicine (2014) revealed that mindfulness meditation reduces negative thinking and stress. Actionable Step: Dedicate five minutes daily to a guided meditation that focuses on releasing negativity.

2. Journaling: Writing down thoughts allows for reflection and emotional release. Actionable Step: Try the "Write and Rip" method. Write down your toxic

thoughts and physically destroy the paper as a symbolic release.

3. Gratitude Practice: Gratitude counteracts negativity by shifting focus to positive experiences. Actionable Step: End each day by listing three things you're grateful for and why.

Real-Life Story

Priya, a college student, found herself trapped in a cycle of negative self-talk after failing an exam. By incorporating meditation and gratitude journaling into her routine, Priya shifted her mindset and regained confidence. Her story exemplifies the power of mental detox techniques.

Positive Surroundings: The Role of Environment in Fostering Joy

Our surroundings significantly influence our mental state. A positive environment can serve as a buffer against negativity and a source of inspiration.

Designing a Positive Environment

1. Declutter Your Space: A clutter-free environment promotes mental clarity. Actionable Step: Spend 10 minutes daily organizing a specific area in your home or workspace.

2. Surround Yourself with Positive People: The company you keep shapes your mindset. Actionable Step: Schedule regular interactions with uplifting friends or mentors.

3. Digital Minimalism: Reduce exposure to negative content online. Cal Newport's book Digital Minimalism highlights how intentional screen use enhances mental well-being. Actionable Step: Implement a "Tech-Free Hour" each evening to unwind.

Scientific Insight

A Harvard study spanning 80 years found that strong, positive relationships are the greatest predictors of happiness. By cultivating supportive connections, we create a network that fosters joy and resilience.

Real-Life Example

Nina, a graphic designer, found herself overwhelmed by the negativity of social media. By adopting digital minimalism and spending more time in nature, she improved her mental health and creativity. Nina's transformation underscores the role of environment in shaping our outlook.

Conclusion: Embracing Positivity for a Brighter Future

Breaking free from negativity is not an overnight process but a journey of consistent effort and self-awareness. By identifying and reframing negative patterns, detoxifying your mind, and fostering positive surroundings, you can create a life rooted in joy and possibility.

Anna, Mark, Priya, and Nina's stories illustrate that transformation is within reach for anyone willing to take actionable steps. With the insights and practices shared in this chapter, you are equipped to shed the weight of negativity and embrace a brighter, more fulfilling future.

Resources for Further Reading

1. Seligman, M. E. P. (2006). Learned Optimism: How to Change Your Mind and Your Life.

2. Emmons, R. A. (2007). Thanks!: How the New Science of Gratitude Can Make You Happier.

3. Fredrickson, B. L. (2009). Positivity: Discover the Upward Spiral That Will Change Your Life.

4. Kabat-Zinn, J. (1990). Full Catastrophe Living: Using the Wisdom of Your Body and Mind to Face Stress, Pain, and Illness.

5. Newport, C. (2019). Digital Minimalism: Choosing a Focused Life in a Noisy World.

6. Harvard Study of Adult Development. (2017). "Good Genes Are Nice, But Joy Is Better." Harvard Gazette.

7. Beck, A. T. (1979). Cognitive Therapy and the Emotional Disorders.

8. Brown, B. (2015). Daring Greatly: How the Courage

to Be Vulnerable Transforms the Way We Live, Love, Parent, and Lead.

9. Clear, J. (2018). Atomic Habits: An Easy & Proven Way to Build Good Habits & Break Bad Ones.

10. Tolle, E. (2004). The Power of Now: A Guide to Spiritual Enlightenment.

CHAPTER 4

REWIRING YOUR MIND FOR SUCCESS

"The greatest discovery of my generation is that a human being can alter his life by altering his attitudes." — William James

Introduction: Transforming Your Mindset for Success

In the fast-paced world we live in, it's easy to believe that success is something determined by external forces — luck, timing, or circumstances beyond our control. However, what if we told you that the key to achieving success lies within the very structure of your brain? That's right — your mind is more than just a passive observer of life's events. With the right tools, you can actually "rewire" your brain, creating a mindset that not only embraces success but actively works toward it.

This chapter will explore how you can harness the power of neuroplasticity to reshape your thoughts and actions, build habits that propel you toward success, and transform your internal dialogue into a tool for growth and positivity. We'll dive into practical techniques like morning rituals, nightly reflections, affirmations, visualization, and the power of self-talk to help you start building a success-oriented mindset today.

Key Insights: The Neuroplasticity Advantage and How to Use It

The Brain's Incredible Ability to Change: Neuroplasticity

One of the most exciting discoveries in modern neuroscience is neuroplasticity — the brain's ability to reorganize itself by forming new neural connections throughout life. Simply put, your brain is not a static organ. It has the power to change in response to the thoughts, actions, and experiences you expose it to. This ability is particularly crucial for habit formation and mindset change.

Dr. Norman Doidge, in his book The Brain That Changes Itself, highlights several real-life examples of individuals who have used neuroplasticity to recover from traumatic brain injuries and psychological challenges. These cases illustrate that with the right kind of mental training, people can not only heal their brains but also strengthen them. This research forms the basis for a powerful argument: you can rewire your brain to embrace success through intentional practices, no matter where you're starting from.

In one compelling case, a woman named Sarah suffered from chronic anxiety and depression that held her back from achieving her professional and personal goals. After years of struggling, she embarked on a cognitive-behavioral therapy (CBT) program that taught her to recognize and challenge negative thoughts. Over time, Sarah rewired her brain's neural pathways, replacing anxiety with confidence and negative self-talk with affirmations of self-worth. The results were profound: she became more successful at work and experienced a newfound sense of peace in her personal life. The evidence from Sarah's transformation, combined with scientific research, demonstrates that the brain's capacity for change is vast and can be harnessed for success.

Building Positive Habits: From Morning Rituals to Nightly Reflections

One of the most effective ways to rewire your brain for success is by consciously building positive habits that serve as the foundation for your day. Morning rituals and nightly reflections are two powerful strategies that can prime your mind for the challenges and opportunities of each day.

1. Morning Rituals: The way you start your day sets the tone for everything that follows. According to research by Shawn Achor, author of The Happiness Advantage, practicing small positive habits in the morning — such as gratitude, meditation, or physical exercise — can boost productivity, increase happiness, and foster a positive outlook on life. The key is consistency: over time, these rituals help create neural pathways associated with optimism and focus, making it easier to approach the day with a success-oriented mindset.

A real-life example is John, a corporate executive who was struggling to keep up with the demands of his job. He felt overwhelmed and stressed, affecting his performance and overall satisfaction. After reading about the impact of morning rituals, John decided to experiment with a 20-minute morning routine that included deep breathing, a short meditation, and a focus on gratitude. Within a few weeks, he noticed a significant change in his energy levels, clarity, and stress management. The consistency of these rituals slowly rewired his brain to approach challenges with a more balanced, success-driven mindset.

2. Nightly Reflections: Just as your morning sets the tone for the day, your evening rituals can influence your mindset as you wind down. Taking a few minutes to reflect on your achievements, express gratitude, and visualize your goals can help solidify the habits you've worked on during the day. According to Dr. John C. Norcross, a leading expert in habit formation, writing down daily reflections promotes deeper neural encoding of positive experiences, making it easier for them to become a natural part of your mindset.

Rachel, a successful entrepreneur, made nightly reflection a non-negotiable part of her routine. Before bed, she would take a few minutes to write down three things she was grateful for and reflect on her wins, no matter how small. This practice helped her shift her focus from stress and self-doubt to appreciation and forward momentum. Over time, Rachel's nightly reflections helped rewire her brain to prioritize positive outcomes and gratitude, making her more resilient and focused on success.

Affirmations and Visualization: Tools for a Success-Oriented Mindset

The power of thought is undeniable. Research shows that repeated positive affirmations and vivid visualizations can trigger changes in the brain, encouraging new thought patterns that align with your goals.

1. Affirmations: Affirmations are positive statements that you repeat to yourself with the intention of changing your beliefs and thought patterns. A study published in the Social Cognitive and Affective Neuroscience journal found that affirmations activate the brain's reward centers, making individuals feel more confident and focused on their goals. This phenomenon is known as "self-affirmation theory," and it suggests that by affirming your values and strengths, you can overcome self-doubt and increase motivation.

Consider David, a professional athlete who struggled with performance anxiety before big competitions. He began using affirmations like, "I am focused, confident, and capable of succeeding." Over time, this simple habit helped David feel more empowered and less nervous, contributing to his improved performance. The power of affirmations lies in their ability to change your brain's habitual patterns, shifting you from a mindset of fear to one of confidence and capability.

2. Visualization: Visualization is the process of imagining yourself achieving a specific goal or living the life you desire. Research by Dr. Denise C. Park, a professor at the University of Texas, suggests that mental rehearsal through visualization can enhance performance by reinforcing the neural pathways involved in actual physical practice. Athletes, for example, frequently use visualization techniques to mentally rehearse their performances before competing. But this technique isn't limited to sports; anyone can use visualization to mentally prepare for a successful outcome in any area of life.

Ava, a manager at a large tech company, began visualizing herself leading her team to a successful project launch. Every morning before work, she would close her eyes and imagine herself navigating challenges with ease, receiving praise from her colleagues, and feeling a deep sense of accomplishment. After several months of this practice, Ava noticed that she began to perform at a higher level, handling stress better and achieving her goals with confidence. Visualization had rewired her brain to approach her work with a success-oriented mindset.

The Power of Self-Talk: Speaking Positivity into Existence

One of the most influential tools for success is self-talk — the internal dialogue you have with yourself throughout the day. Negative self-talk can reinforce limiting beliefs and hinder your ability to take risks and pursue your goals. Conversely, positive self-talk can motivate you to take action, build resilience, and cultivate the mindset needed for success.

Studies have shown that athletes who use positive self-talk experience reduced anxiety and improved performance. For instance, a study published in Psychology of Sport and Exercise found that athletes who used positive self-talk before competitions performed significantly better than those who engaged in negative self-talk. Similarly, a study from the Journal of Personality and Social Psychology found that individuals who practiced positive self-talk were more likely to achieve their personal and professional goals.

A practical way to begin using self-talk for success is to catch yourself when you start to engage in negative thoughts. Replace statements like, "I can't do this" or "I'm not good enough" with empowering alternatives like, "I am capable of achieving this" or "I am learning and growing every day." Over time, this shift will retrain your brain to focus on your potential rather than your limitations.

Conclusion: Creating a Success-Oriented Mindset

The concept of rewiring your brain for success is not just theoretical — it is grounded in science, supported by research, and demonstrated in the lives of countless individuals who have transformed their habits, mindsets, and lives. By understanding the power of neuroplasticity and implementing strategies like positive morning rituals, nightly reflections, affirmations, visualization, and self-talk, you can begin to rewire your brain to embrace success.

The journey to a success-oriented mindset is a gradual one, but every small step you take makes a significant difference.

Start by integrating one or two practices into your daily routine, and gradually build upon them. Keep track of your progress and remember that setbacks are part of the process — they do not define your ability to succeed.

Resources for Further Reading

1. Doidge, N. (2007). The Brain That Changes Itself: Stories of Personal Triumph from the Frontiers of Brain Science. Viking Penguin.

2. Achor, S. (2010). The Happiness Advantage: The Seven Principles of Positive Psychology That Fuel Success and Performance at Work. Crown Business.

3. Norcross, J. C. (2011). Changeology: 5 Steps to Realizing Your Goals and Resolutions. TarcherPerigee.

4. Seligman, M. E. P. (2011). Learned Optimism: How to Change Your Mind and Your Life. Vintage.

5. Neff, K. D. (2011). Self-Compassion: The Proven Power of Being Kind to Yourself. William Morrow.

6. Park, D. C. (2010). The Benefits of Mental Rehearsal and Visualization: How Imagining Success

Can Lead to Real Success. Psychology Today.

7. Hardy, D. (2013). The Power of Positive Self-Talk. Journal of Personality and Social Psychology.

CHAPTER 5

LIVING JOYFULLY EVERY DAY

"Joy is not in things; it is in us." — Richard Wagner

Introduction: Choosing Joy Every Day

In a world that often feels overwhelmed with pressures and uncertainties, it can be difficult to find and maintain joy. We're frequently told that joy comes from big accomplishments, financial success, or the ideal circumstances — but what if the real secret lies not in these external factors but in how we choose to experience life every day? What if happiness wasn't something to wait for, but something we could cultivate through our choices, mindset, and actions?

This chapter explores how to live joyfully every day by embracing the concept of a "joy mindset," celebrating small wins, practicing self-compassion, and remaining consistent in the pursuit of happiness, even during challenging times. You'll discover how adopting a joyful approach to life can lead to lasting happiness and improved well-being, no matter what life throws your way.

Key Insights: The Joy Mindset and How to Cultivate It

The Joy Mindset: Choosing Happiness as a Daily Practice

At the heart of living joyfully is a mindset — a deliberate choice to seek happiness and fulfillment, even in the midst of ordinary, sometimes difficult, circumstances. According to positive psychology expert Dr. Martin Seligman, happiness is a skill that can be cultivated, much like a muscle. It's not about waiting for a "perfect" moment or a big change; it's about consciously choosing joy every day.

A real-life example of someone who embodies the joy mindset is Linda, a corporate manager who, despite facing constant work-related stress, decided to shift her focus. Rather than wait for a promotion or external validation to feel happiness, Linda committed to practicing daily gratitude. She set aside time each morning to list three things she was grateful for, no matter how small. This simple act reprogrammed her brain to focus on the positive aspects of her life, allowing her to experience a greater sense of joy and satisfaction in her daily routine.

Research by Dr. Barbara Fredrickson, a pioneer in the field of positive psychology, supports this. Fredrickson's broaden-and-build theory suggests that positive emotions like joy help us build resilience and coping mechanisms, enhancing our ability to deal with life's challenges. By consciously choosing happiness every day, we essentially train our brains to see the world through a more joyful lens.

The Art of Celebration: Finding Joy in Small Wins

In our society, success is often measured by major milestones — promotions, weddings, awards, or other big achievements.

However, focusing only on these large events can lead us to overlook the small, everyday wins that are crucial for our overall well-being and happiness. Finding joy in these small victories is an art, and it's one that can significantly enhance our experience of life.

Celebrating small wins doesn't just bring joy in the moment; it also reinforces positive behaviors, which can lead to long-term success. For instance, a study published in the Journal of Positive Psychology found that celebrating small victories is directly linked to higher levels of motivation and productivity. Each small win acts as a reminder that progress is happening, even if it's not always immediately visible.

Consider James, a writer who was struggling to finish his novel. Instead of waiting for the completion of the entire book to celebrate, he began celebrating small milestones, like finishing a chapter or writing 500 words. By acknowledging these smaller achievements, James was able to stay motivated and maintain a sense of progress, even when the end goal seemed far off. The joy of each small win kept him going, ultimately helping him finish the novel and share it with the world.

Finding joy in small wins isn't just about external achievements — it's about acknowledging the efforts we make every day. Whether it's completing a task at work, sticking to a fitness routine, or simply being kind to someone, these small victories deserve to be celebrated. By making a habit of recognizing and celebrating them, you create a positive feedback loop that fosters joy and motivation.

The Role of Self-Compassion: Being Kind to Yourself

One of the most profound ways to sustain joy is through self-compassion — treating yourself with the same kindness and understanding that you would extend to a close friend. In a culture that often promotes perfectionism and achievement at all costs, we can easily become our own harshest critics. But self-compassion offers a powerful antidote to this inner negativity, enabling us to navigate challenges with greater ease and kindness.

Research by Dr. Kristin Neff, one of the leading researchers on self-compassion, shows that individuals who practice self-compassion have higher levels of emotional resilience, less anxiety, and greater overall life satisfaction. By embracing self-compassion, we allow ourselves to experience joy without judgment, even during tough times.

A powerful real-life example of self-compassion is Ella, a woman who faced severe burnout after juggling multiple roles as a mother, career woman, and volunteer. Feeling overwhelmed and exhausted, Ella made the decision to shift her approach by practicing self-compassion. She began to treat herself with care and understanding, taking breaks when needed and forgiving herself for not always being "perfect." Slowly but surely, this shift in mindset helped Ella reclaim her joy and energy, enabling her to handle life's demands more effectively.

Self-compassion allows us to accept our imperfections, learn from our mistakes, and move forward with a sense of grace. By being kind to ourselves, we create a nurturing environment for joy to thrive, even during challenging moments.

Consistency Is Key: How to Sustain Joy Amid Challenges

Joy is not a fleeting emotion; it's a sustainable mindset that can be maintained over time with consistency and intention. Life will inevitably present obstacles — unexpected setbacks, tough days, or even long periods of struggle. However, consistency in your joyful practices can help you maintain a sense of well-being, even when life gets tough.

The key to sustaining joy is building habits that support your well-being. According to Dr. Sonja Lyubomirsky, author of The How of Happiness, habits such as expressing gratitude, engaging in acts of kindness, and cultivating optimism can help you stay resilient in the face of adversity. These habits create a foundation of positivity that allows joy to endure, regardless of external circumstances.

One person who exemplifies this is Carlos, a man who had faced several personal losses over the years. While he was grieving, Carlos committed to maintaining a daily gratitude practice, writing down three things he was thankful for each day. This habit helped him slowly reframe his perspective, allowing him to find small moments of joy even in the midst of sorrow. Over time, this consistency in focusing on gratitude became a powerful tool for emotional resilience, helping him recover more quickly from his grief and continue moving forward with a joyful outlook.

Consistency in joyful habits doesn't mean ignoring pain or pretending that everything is always fine. It's about intentionally nurturing a mindset that allows joy to coexist with life's challenges. By committing to practices that cultivate happiness on a daily basis, you can maintain a steady source of joy — even when things don't go as planned.

Conclusion: The Practice of Joyful Living

Living joyfully every day is a choice — one that requires intentionality, self-compassion, and consistency. By embracing a joy mindset, celebrating small wins, practicing self-compassion, and remaining consistent in your pursuit of happiness, you can create a life that's full of meaning and fulfillment.

Remember that joy isn't something that will magically appear once you reach a certain milestone or achieve a specific goal. It's a daily practice that can be cultivated through simple actions, like starting each day with gratitude, celebrating your efforts, being kind to yourself, and staying consistent in your pursuit of happiness. Each small step you take toward living joyfully makes a significant difference in your overall well-being and success.

Resources for Further Reading

1. Seligman, M. E. P. (2002). Authentic Happiness:

Using the New Positive Psychology to Realize Your Potential for Lasting Fulfillment. Free Press.

2. Neff, K. D. (2011). Self-Compassion: The Proven Power of Being Kind to Yourself. William Morrow.

3. Fredrickson, B. L. (2009). Positivity: Top-Notch Research Reveals the Upward Spiral That Will Change Your Life. Crown.

4. Lyubomirsky, S. (2008). The How of Happiness: A New Approach to Getting the Life You Want. Penguin Press.

5. Achor, S. (2010). The Happiness Advantage: The Seven Principles of Positive Psychology That Fuel Success and Performance at Work. Crown Business.

6. Fredrickson, B. L. (2001). The Broaden-and-Build Theory of Positive Emotions. American Psychologist.

7. Lyubomirsky, S., & Sheldon, K. M. (2005). Pursuing Happiness: The Architecture of Sustainable Change. Review of General Psychology.

8. Gable, S. L., & Haidt, J. (2005). What (and Why) Is Positive Psychology?. Review of General Psychology.

9. Cameron, J. (1998). The Artist's Way: A Spiritual Path to Higher Creativity. Jeremy P. Tarcher.

CHAPTER 6

THE RIPPLE EFFECT OF POSITIVITY

"The best way to find yourself is to lose yourself in the service of others." — Mahatma Gandhi

Introduction: The Power of Positive Energy

Imagine for a moment that your mood, energy, and actions have the power to affect those around you. What if every smile, act of kindness, or positive interaction you have could create a ripple effect that spreads far beyond your immediate circle? This chapter is all about the transformative power of positivity — not just how it impacts you, but how it extends outward, influencing the world in profound ways.

The ripple effect of positivity suggests that the more we practice kindness, gratitude, and joy, the more we inspire others to do the same. From creating supportive communities to fostering connections and sharing moments of kindness, we have the potential to generate a cycle of positivity that can spread throughout society. In this chapter, we explore how to harness the ripple effect, from spreading joy through your own actions to building supportive networks and embracing the joy of giving.

Key Insights: The Ripple Effect and Its Profound Impact

Spreading Joy: Impacting Others with Your Positive Energy

The idea of spreading joy through your energy isn't just wishful thinking — it's supported by scientific research and real-life examples. Emotions are contagious, and positivity can be as infectious as negativity. A study by Dr. Nicholas Christakis at Harvard University found that emotions, including happiness and joy, can spread through social networks, often affecting people you don't even know directly.

This means that your positive energy doesn't just impact your immediate interactions, but it can ripple out to others in your community, workplace, or social circle.

Take the example of Eva, a schoolteacher who started each day by greeting her students with an enthusiastic smile and a word of encouragement. Over time, she noticed a shift in the class's dynamic. Students became more engaged, kind to one another, and showed more empathy. Even on days when the class faced challenges, the positive energy Eva exuded set the tone for others to follow. Eva's ability to spread joy created an environment of positivity that reached beyond her own actions, fostering a culture of kindness and collaboration in her classroom.

Research from the Journal of Personality and Social Psychology also suggests that positive emotions, such as joy and gratitude, trigger a "social contagion" effect. This means that when we share joy, it's more likely to be passed along, creating a chain reaction of positive energy. The more we engage in positive actions, the more we influence the emotions and behaviors of others, often without even realizing it.

Community and Connection: Building a Supportive Network

A supportive community can amplify the effects of positivity, creating an environment where everyone feels empowered to practice kindness and gratitude. Humans are social creatures, and the connections we form with others play a critical role in our well-being. When we surround ourselves with people who share similar values and uplift us, we strengthen the positive impact on our lives and the lives of those around us.

Building a supportive network isn't just about seeking positivity for ourselves; it's about creating an ecosystem where others can thrive as well. Take Michael, for example, who worked for a non-profit organization. He made it a priority to build strong connections with his coworkers by offering support and encouragement, both professionally and personally. Through this practice, Michael cultivated an environment of trust and compassion within his team, where everyone felt valued and connected. As a result, the organization experienced increased collaboration, improved morale, and a deeper sense of community.

The role of community is also seen in research by Dr. Julianne Holt-Lunstad, who found that individuals with strong social connections tend to live longer, healthier lives. A supportive network doesn't just provide emotional strength; it enhances physical and mental well-being, reinforcing the notion that positive relationships create a ripple effect of health and happiness.

Gratitude Beyond Self: The Joy of Giving and Acts of Kindness

One of the most powerful ways to create a ripple effect of positivity is through acts of kindness and giving. When we express gratitude and give to others, it not only benefits the recipient, but it also boosts our own sense of joy and satisfaction. The simple act of giving can trigger a cascade of positive emotions, not just in us, but in those we interact with as well.

Take Sarah, who decided to volunteer at a local shelter every weekend. At first, she thought of it as a way to give back to her community, but she soon realized the profound impact it had on her own well-being. Not only did she witness the direct effects of her kindness on others, but she also found that her own mood and outlook on life significantly improved. By being part of something bigger than herself, Sarah experienced an increased sense of purpose and fulfillment. She, in turn, inspired others in her community to volunteer, creating a ripple of kindness that spread far beyond her initial act.

Research by Dr. Stephen Post, author of Why Good Things Happen to Good People, shows that giving and kindness not only enhance the well-being of others, but they also promote our own happiness. Acts of kindness have been shown to increase levels of dopamine and oxytocin, neurotransmitters associated with happiness and connection, further fueling the cycle of positivity.

The Infinite Cycle of Joy: How Positive Actions Create a Better World

The ripple effect of positivity doesn't stop with one act of kindness or joy. It creates an infinite cycle where each positive interaction begets another, ultimately leading to a more compassionate, supportive, and joyful world. This infinite cycle can be seen in every corner of society — from the way communities support one another in times of crisis to the small, everyday gestures that brighten someone's day.

A powerful example of this is seen in the concept of "paying it forward," where an act of kindness inspires the recipient to pass on the kindness to someone else. A study conducted by Dr. Michael Norton at Harvard Business School found that people who receive acts of kindness are more likely to engage in kind acts themselves. This creates a ripple effect of kindness, contributing to a culture of giving and support.

Moreover, this cycle isn't limited to just individual actions. When we collectively contribute to a positive environment, whether at work, in our neighborhoods, or on a global scale, the impact grows exponentially. Positive social movements, environmental efforts, and community outreach programs all function as part of this cycle, amplifying the effects of individual acts of kindness.

As we embrace the cycle of joy, we create an environment where kindness and positivity become the norm, rather than the exception. This not only improves our own lives but contributes to a world that is more compassionate, supportive, and connected.

Conclusion: The Power of Positivity to Transform the World

The ripple effect of positivity is a reminder that our actions, no matter how small, have the power to create lasting change. By spreading joy, building supportive communities, practicing gratitude, and giving selflessly, we set off a chain reaction that transforms lives and society as a whole. The more we engage in positive actions, the more we inspire others to do the same, creating an infinite cycle of joy that can ultimately lead to a better world.

The ripple effect shows us that we don't need to wait for a grand event or milestone to make a difference. By committing to positivity every day, we can influence the world around us in ways we never imagined. Our energy, actions, and mindset can inspire others, creating a community and culture where kindness and joy flourish.

Resources for Further Reading

1. Christakis, N. A., & Fowler, J. H. (2009). Connected: The Surprising Power of Our Social Networks and How They Shape Our Lives. Back Bay Books.

2. Post, S. G. (2007). Why Good Things Happen to Good People: How to Live a Longer, Healthier, Happier Life by the Simple Act of Giving. Broadway Books.

3. Holt-Lunstad, J., Smith, T. B., & Layton, J. B. (2010). Social Relationships and Mortality Risk: A Meta-Analytic Review. PLoS Medicine.

4. Fredrickson, B. L. (2009). Positivity: Top-Notch Research Reveals the Upward Spiral That Will Change Your Life. Crown.

5. Lyubomirsky, S. (2007). The How of Happiness: A New Approach to Getting the Life You Want. Penguin Press.

6. Achor, S. (2010). The Happiness Advantage: The Seven Principles of Positive Psychology That Fuel Success and Performance at Work. Crown Business.

7. Norton, M. I., et al. (2007). "Spreading the Wealth: The Effect of Generosity on Subsequent Generosity." Psychological Science.

8. Cameron, J. (1998). The Artist's Way: A Spiritual

Path to Higher Creativity. Jeremy P. Tarcher.

CONCLUSION: YOUR JOURNEY TO EVERLASTING JOY

"Joy does not simply happen to us. We have to choose it and keep choosing it every day." — Henri J.M. Nouwen

Recap of Key Insights: What You've Learned

As we conclude this exploration into the science of happiness, it's important to take a moment to reflect on the key insights we've uncovered. From the foundational understanding of positivity and its effects on our well-being to the actionable steps you can take to cultivate happiness in your life, this journey has equipped you with tools and knowledge to unlock lasting joy.

You've learned that happiness isn't a fleeting emotion but a state of being that can be nurtured through intentional practices. We explored the power of positive thinking, the importance of gratitude, and how small daily habits, like mindfulness and self-compassion, can radically transform your outlook on life. The ripple effect of positivity shows that the energy we radiate doesn't just affect us; it has the potential to create waves of joy in our relationships and communities.

Most importantly, we've highlighted that joy is a choice — one that we can make every day. By embracing simple practices and positive psychology principles, we can shift our mindset, break free from negativity, and cultivate a life full of happiness, resilience, and connection.

Embracing a Joyful Life: Moving Forward with Positivity

The path to a joyful life begins with intention. Now that you've gained insight into the science of happiness, it's time to put these principles into practice. The tools and strategies discussed in this book are not meant to be passive information but actionable steps to create real, lasting change.

Start by incorporating small, consistent habits into your daily routine. Whether it's taking a few moments to express gratitude, engaging in physical activity to boost your mood, or practicing mindfulness to calm your mind, these practices will soon become second nature. Surround yourself with people who uplift and support you, and make positivity contagious by sharing kindness and encouragement with others.

Remember, life is not about being happy all the time. It's about creating an environment and mindset that allows joy to flourish, even in the face of challenges. When difficult moments arise, lean into the practices that bring you peace and balance. Over time, you'll find that joy becomes less of an occasional experience and more of a consistent presence in your life.

A Daily Joy Checklist: Simple Reminders for a Happier You

To make happiness a daily practice, here's a simple checklist to keep you on track:

1. **Morning Gratitude**: Take a moment to list three things you're grateful for. It could be something big or small, but starting your day with gratitude sets a positive tone.

2. **Mindful Breathing**: Spend at least five minutes focused on your breath. Whether it's through meditation or deep breathing exercises, calming your mind can help you stay centered.

3. **Positive Self-Talk**: Be kind to yourself. Replace self-criticism with affirmations that encourage self-love and empowerment.

4. **Acts of Kindness**: Perform at least one small act of kindness each day — whether it's a compliment, helping someone, or simply being there for a friend in need.

5. **Celebrate Small Wins**: Acknowledge your achievements, no matter how minor they may seem. Celebrate the process, not just the outcome.

6. **Reflect Before Bed**: End your day with a reflection on something positive that happened. This helps

train your mind to focus on the good, even on tough days.

The Future Awaits: Your Next Steps in Positive Psychology

The journey toward everlasting joy doesn't end here. In fact, this is only the beginning. By continuing to apply the principles of positive psychology, you'll find that joy becomes more than just a concept; it becomes a way of life. Remember that the future is shaped by the choices you make today. So, as you move forward, make happiness your guiding force, even when the road gets tough.

Take the tools you've learned, and use them to create a ripple effect of joy in your life and in the lives of others. Whether it's through self-compassion, spreading positivity, or connecting with those who support your growth, you are the architect of your own happiness. The future holds endless possibilities for those who choose joy, and it's up to you to embrace it wholeheartedly.

As you embark on this new chapter, keep this one simple truth in mind: **Happiness isn't a destination; it's a jour-**

ney. With every step, you have the power to cultivate joy, inspire others, and create a life that feels truly fulfilling. Here's to the joy-filled future that awaits you.

Resources for Further Reading

1. Lyubomirsky, S. (2007). *The How of Happiness: A New Approach to Getting the Life You Want*. Penguin Press.

2. Achor, S. (2010). *The Happiness Advantage: The Seven Principles of Positive Psychology That Fuel Success and Performance at Work*. Crown Business.

3. Fredrickson, B. L. (2009). *Positivity: Top-Notch Research Reveals the Upward Spiral That Will Change Your Life*. Crown.

4. Cameron, J. (1998). *The Artist's Way: A Spiritual Path to Higher Creativity*. Jeremy P. Tarcher.

5. Seligman, M. E. P. (2002). *Authentic Happiness: Using the New Positive Psychology to Realize Your Potential for Lasting Fulfillment*. Free Press.

6. Neff, K. (2011). *Self-Compassion: The Proven Power*

of Being Kind to Yourself. William Morrow.

7. Emmons, R. A., & McCullough, M. E. (2003). *Counting Blessings versus Burdens: An Experimental Investigation of Gratitude and Subjective Well-Being in Daily Life. Journal of Personality and Social Psychology.*

8. Grant, A. (2013). *Give and Take: A Revolutionary Approach to Success.* Viking.

MAY I ASK YOU FOR A SMALL FAVOR?

I want to express my sincere gratitude for choosing to invest your time in reading this book. Your decision to explore this work among countless others means a lot to me.

I hope that within these pages, you've discovered actionable insights that can enhance your daily life. Your journey doesn't have to end here, though.

May I kindly request an additional 30 seconds of your valuable time?

Sharing your thoughts about the book through a review would be immensely appreciated. Your review serves as a beacon, guiding other readers to take a chance on my books. It's a small gesture that carries significant weight in the world of authors.

To submit your review effortlessly, please click on the link below. It will take you directly to the book's review page:

"The Positive Psychology for Daily Joy"

Alternatively, you can also find the "**Reviews Section**" of this book's page on Amazon.

Your review will require just a minute of your time but will make a monumental difference in helping me connect with a broader audience and I eagerly look forward to reading your review.

Once again, thank you for your unwavering support of my work.

DISCLAIMER

This book is for educational purposes only. Readers acknowledge that the author does not render legal, financial, medical, or professional advice. The content within this book has been derived from various sources. Please consult a licensed professional before attempting any techniques outlined in this book.

By reading this document, the reader agrees that under no circumstances is the author responsible for any direct or indirect losses incurred as a result of the use of the information contained within this document, including but not limited to errors, omissions, or inaccuracies.

Adherence to all applicable laws and regulations, including international, federal, state, and local governing professional licensing, business practices, advertising, and all other jurisdictions, is the sole responsibility of the purchaser or reader.

Neither the author nor the publisher assumes any responsibility or liability whatsoever on behalf of the purchaser or reader of these materials. Any perceived slight of any individual or organization is purely unintentional.

www.ingramcontent.com/pod-product-compliance
Lightning Source LLC
Chambersburg PA
CBHW061250250726
48653CB00002B/597